VOODOO INVERSO

The Felix Pollak Prize in Poetry

Voodoo Inverso

MARK WAGENAAR

THE UNIVERSITY OF WISCONSIN PRESS

THE UNIVERSITY OF WISCONSIN PRESS

1930 Monroe Street, 3rd Floor
Madison, Wisconsin 53711-2059
uwpress.wisc.edu

3 Henrietta Street
London WCE 8LU, England
eurospanbookstore.com

Library of Congress Cataloging-in-Publication Data
Wagenaar, Mark.
    Voodoo inverso / Mark Wagenaar.
       p.   cm. -- (The Felix Pollak prize in poetry)
    Poems.
    ISBN 978-0-299-28814-3 (pbk. : alk. paper) -- ISBN 978-0-299-28813-6 (e-book)
    I. Title. II. Series: Felix Pollak prize in poetry (Series)
    PS3623.A3523V66<M#>2012
    811'.6--dc23
                                  2011041956

CONTENTS

PART III   *Aubades & Nocturnes*

ACKNOWLEDGMENTS

THE AUTHOR would like to offer his gratitude and thanks to these magazines that first published the following poems:

Adirondack Review: "Elegiac Stanzas" (as "A Prophet Dies on the Day He Predicted"), "Unknowable Aubade"

American Literary Review: "Portrait of the Artist with Dante"

Antioch Review: "Gacela of the Wounds"

Apalachee Review: "Deer Hour Gospel," "Thinking of Thomas à Kempis on a Fall Evening"

Atlanta Review: "Gacela of the Bright Omen"

Bellingham Review: "Film 101: Final Exam"

Chiron Review: "Dusk Hour Gospel (Each Poem Is a Poem of Exile)"

Cider Press Review: "A Blessing"

Colorado Review: "Sixth Finger Gospel"

Columbia: A Journal of Literature and Art: "Nocturne Past Dreaming"

Connecticut River Review: "The Other Side of the Curtain" (as "I'll Know the Title Next Time I Hear the Train Whistle")

Copper Nickel: "Tulip Mania (The New Numerology)," "The Disciples Question
Their Yogi"

Crab Creek Review: "Since You Asked" (as "Letter Home 2")

Crab Orchard Review: "Six Prayer Kites over Rock Island"

Dogwood: "A Parade of Ghosts"

Fugue: " 'Raindrop' "

Georgetown Review: "Bayadère Notturno"

Harpur Palate: "Other Equations for Velocity," "Elegy with Two Lemons"

Hiram Poetry Review: "The Joke"

Kestrel: "Reliquaries"

Many Mountains Moving: "Unknowable Nocturne"

Mid-American Review: "Spill," "The History of Your Life in a Hair Strand"

New Delta Review: "Curio"

New England Review: "Errata," "Zen River Travel"

New Ohio Review: "Carnival Nocturne"

Nimrod: "Filament," "The History of Ecstasy"

Ninth Letter: "Sun Goin' Down Bad Luck Blues"

North American Review: "The Way of All Flesh"

Notre Dame Review: "Nocturne: Exit Music for a Film," "The Butcher with Nothing But Bones," "Orpheus amongst the Fishbones"

Oberon Poetry Magazine: "Nocturne of a Thousand & One Notes"

Phoebe: "Early Hymn from Humpback Rock"

South Carolina Review: "Slow Migration Toward Ecstasy"

Southeast Review: "Survival Plans"

Southern Review: "The Litter Bearers (II)" (as "The Litter Bearers"), "Portraits of the Artist with Montale"

Subtropics: "Chiropractic (Bootblacks & Lightbulbs)"

Third Coast: "Bat Hour Gospel"

Yalobusha Review: "Lines for a Thirtieth Birthday," "Revenant"

Yemassee: "Nail Bed Gospel"

32 Poems: "The Other World"

West Branch: "The Litter Bearers," "Moth Hour Gospel," "Self-Portrait of the Artist as Io" (as "Io"), "A Splinter of the Buddha's Tooth," "Voodoo Inverso," "Domestic Nocturne," "Deep Image Hall of Fame"

*"Bat Hour Gospel" was nominated by *Third Coast* for a Pushcart Prize.

* "Bayadère Notturno" is the 2011 runner-up of *Georgetown Review*'s annual contest, and the 2009 runner-up of *Sow's Ear Poetry Review*'s annual contest.

* "Curio" is the 2009 winner of *New Delta Review*'s Matt Clark Poetry Prize.

* "Lines for a Thirtieth Birthday" is the 2009 runner-up of *Yalobusha Review*'s Yellowwood Poetry Prize.

* "Nocturne of a Thousand & One Notes" is the 2011 winner of *Oberon Poetry Magazine*'s annual contest.

* "Nocturne Past Dreaming" is the 2011 winner of *Columbia: A Journal of Literature and Art*'s annual contest.

* "The Other Side of the Curtain" is the 2009 winner of the *Connecticut River Review*'s annual contest.

* " 'Raindrop' " is the 2011 runner-up of *Fugue*'s annual contest.

* "Revenant" is the 2009 winner of *Yalobusha Review*'s Yellowwood Poetry Prize.

* "The Way of All Flesh" is the 2011 second runner-up of *North American Review*'s James Hearst Poetry Prize.

THE AUTHOR would also like to thank the following people for their love, inspiration, friendship, instruction, money, and love: my beloved wife & inspiration, fellow poet and sweetest spirit, first reader & best editor, Chelsea Marie Wagenaar, without whom this book would simply not exist; my dear family: best man Big Fred, Kathy, Jesse, Joshie, Benny, Aldemar, Hooch; my new family: Michele, Marissa, Alaina, and junior groomsman Big Kyler; my extended Canada family: Art & Gertje, who mailed me her translations of poets such as Guido Gezelle, fellow poet Shane Wagenaar, and Uncle Joe; my New Jersey family, Gary & Millie, Gary & Barb, Mike & Joanne, & Stevie; my Texas family, the Blockers: Jayson & Lizzie & Brooklyn, Justin, Jarrod, Jay & Mary; fellow poet Courtney Kampa for her vision, correspondence, and her dear heart; friends old and new: John Van Ryn, Peter DeFeyter, Scottie Lindstrom, Ivan Joseph, Chris Beardie, Tim Regetz, Dave Cianto, Dave Davis, Britt Shivers, Sierra Bellows, Aja Gabel, Bear Grylls, George Tadros, Andrew Bell, Dave Rawbone, Pete Bullette, Wayne Gretzky, Michelle McAlister, and others too numerous to mention; poetry peers for their guidance, kind hearts, generosity, friendship, wisdom, and rounds of drinks: Jane Lewty, Chris Tanseer, Lisa Fay Coutley, Jasmine Bailey, Evan Beaty, George David Clark, Jon Schneider, Julia Hansen, Joe Chapman; my professors: Charles Wright (till water cuts the trail, old friend), Lisa Russ Spaar, Rita Dove, Greg Orr, Jackie Osherow, Bruce Bond, Corey Marks, Pete Fairchild, Paul Guest, Eric Pankey, Jon Wallace, Barb Mesle, Vince Gotera, Rebecca Dunham; the many editors who provided expertise and opportunity, especially John Poch and Jeanne Leiby; the workshops at the University of Virginia, and the University of Utah; Graceland University; the staff at the University of Wisconsin Press, for their time, expertise, and patience: Sheila McMahon, Matthew Cosby, Ron Wallace, Raphael Kadushin, Carla Marolt. A big thank you to Jean Valentine. It's impossible to mention everyone, but my thanks to you all.

The title of this collection was taken from a small billboard in Amsterdam, one of a series to raise awareness about sex trafficking; the title poem is in the voice of this anonymous victim. The cover photo was taken by Melanie Fish at Passion Conference 2012. It's a giant hand made out of everyday items that are still made with slave labor (over $3 million dollars was raised at the conference). Parties interested in contributing to the fight against human trafficking can go to www.268generation.org or www.notforsalecampaign.org.

This book is dedicated to my Lord and Savior, Jesus Christ.

PART I

Self-Portraits & Disappearances

Chiropractic *(Bootblacks & Lightbulbs)*

for Chelsea Wagenaar

Not the massage you were expecting,
but one that parts the many waters
of your back muscles—*latissismus dorsi,*
trapezius, the ones that sound so much
like stars, *rhomboideus minor, iliocostalis*—
until the vertebrae, living stones, sing,
right down to the sacrum—named
the "sacred bone" by the Greeks
because the soul resides there—down
to the coccyx, formed by vestigial
vertebrae & named for the cuckoo's
bill it resembles, & as two hands
memorize each angle until even
the fossae—the small depressions
only the wind knows about—hum
like wineglasses, you sink into a sleep
like waking, a dream like forgetting,
& the answer to the last crossword clue—
what do bootblacks & lightbulbs do—hovers
like a crow over withered fields, unknowable,
& you try to remember the body's
fourteen stations—or was that something
else entirely—is there one for *clavicle,*
for what follows *joy,* one for what sparks
grief, were desire & laughter two halves
of one station, because it feels like they should be,
& where on the list were the ankles' sharp
spurs, or hands holding water, tongue
tasting lemongrass, liver remembering
malbec, none of them the answer that is always
just out of reach, just beyond the misdirection
& sleight-of-hand memory plays, & no, it wasn't Fu
Manchu who wrote *dry creek bed glimpsed*

by lightning, that's ridiculous, it was oh
the look on his face when he saw you
by morning light for the first time, it was something
like a blessing for they who thirst,
something like grace—mercy for the undeserving,
rain where there are no clouds—it was an answer,
in the synapses' electric blue voids, an answer
somewhere in the fault lines of the body, *shine*.

Spill

There are letters you won't begin until the day
your daughter is born, people who won't sleep tonight
until they hear the ghostly clicking of frogs
they've never seen in the fields beyond. Even then sleep
often startles us, like a hand cresting in a sea of faces.
Or your love of unlit bridges, the one over the Chickahominy,
above water long before you realize it, the surprise
of the water that darkens us, that hurries us along by holding us
under. It's that kind of wonder the loon dives into, the nowhere
it makes anywhere, such is its solitude, the shade-sized body
it leaves behind in the water. Like the gibbous moon it surfaces
beneath, a moon that climbs out of the well of itself to give back
all the light it can—you must have spent a long time alone
to look that way, you must have spent most of your life
crossing out that letter, until its palimpsest reads as a history
of your mistakes. What is my only comfort in life
& death, each catechism asks. That I am not my own,
each answers. No wonder the thanksgiving & the leaping deer
in the Song of Songs. And the vineyards, & the beloved.
Petunias, petunias, their scent like Beethoven played backward.
Rust-on-blood purple of the red maple, the linden's
almost peach-soft timber, the shimmering phosphorescence
of the smoke tree, the mimosa's spikes. A pumpkin's
orange blossom like a lone prayer flag, the mile of sun & water
between the dragonfly's damascene wings, the world
we return to without noticing, as a pianist drifts in
on the airwaves, oscillating in & out of static. A medley
from Pachelbel to U2, how a century can turn between
the pulsing of tendons, how a year can go by after an embrace
before you think of a clever thing to say. A lifetime can pass
in the time it takes a milkweed to spill, for you to find
the name of your daughter among the host of starry parachutes,
though she still sleeps somewhere in your shadow, as you awake,
miles over water, clutching a piece of paper with no words on it.

The History of Ecstasy

Caravaggio, *The Ecstasy of St. Francis*

Everything in freefall through the trees,
blue phloxed & dahliaed as they land,
the flowers we see like sunspots after we close
our eyes. The heart of the wren has an oculus
that lets in only rain, or so its song tells us,
& you've meditated on it so long, the acetylene
milk-starred wren's heart, nine-sided & sailed,
you hear the rustling of its wings each time the drops
begin to fall. In the dark each night the carillonneur
of starlight begins to play, the same two tones
pulsing endlessly, the song of the burning shirt,
the dark buttonhole the nipple slips through.
Where in the tendons & slender muscles
is that memory stored, that has her hands
on that first chord without noticing when she
sits before the keys? Like a dowser staring
at Sahara sand, hands trembling. It's a love
passed down in the bones that has people,
even under gunfire, taking the time to bury
their saints' relics beneath the second willow
at the river's edge. It's something passed
from her mother that has my mother awake
most of the night, trying a last glass of port,
Tylenol 3, chamomile, tryptophan, & finally
Ambien, a bell-sound always between her & sleep.
And so the Italians discover Caravaggio
in their blood, that heart so full of terrible echoes,
the history of the ecstasy of St. Francis
in their palm prints. Though paradise might mean
unbridled joy, who can say if we'd know it when
we found it, or if we'd find our way back again—
the same ecstasy might be somewhere in our own,
if we're willing to bear the wounds.

I know by the ache that water is rising from the soil,
that storms will soon race over the ridgeline
into the valley, each about the size of the town
I grew up in, each with a day's worth of water if it fell
only into each of our palms, spilling into each corner
of our lives. Listen: the sound of wings, the peace that sleep
follows, small mercies, the first drops beginning to fall.

Errata

for dogwood blossom read burning city
for the wings of luna moths
read pointe shoes hung by their ribbons
for mother's hand read shade
the particles that pass right
through your bones
read bracelet of hair on your wrist
each set of bird tracks a new language
(different symbols different songs
for Goldberg Variations read sparrows' flights)
if every language is dying
(each god each capillary each rock
carried from the river & inscribed)
each time your tongue goes dry
it's raining on the ruins of Babel
each time your hands tremble
your mother is calling your name
the faint stars her hair her ashen hair
for the body cross
of the spine & shoulder blades
read the atlas of grief
each living stone

Voodoo Inverso *(Self-Portrait)*

A potion to reverse my trafficker's curse would have the dust
of the streets of Port-au-Prince
or Amsterdam—gourdes or euros, they are no different.

Peonies, because they were the favorite of Pissaro's wife,
& she knew something of being displaced
                                    by misdirected longing.

A drop of the exact color of that longing, how it clings
like acrid millsmoke to skin.

One of the birch leaves floating on the river,
a constellation the drowned must look on in wonder.

A strand of my mother's hair.
There she is now, in her white nightgown,
walking through the empty house

window to window
            (through the white curtains, a feather from one of the crows

flying away from the dawn, rags of the night's shroud in their beaks).

No, it's the moon in the canal below.
Like seeing myself behind a glass door

                        (I'm breadline & moondog,
a line paid out in the deep.

I wait to disappear as a well waits
for the once-a-day brilliance of high noon).

Slow Migration Toward Ecstasy

A year passes between hiccups, another between
the verbs *forgive* & *forget*, & sure enough the moon's
drifted an inch & a half away, then another inch
& a half, its tug on the nape of my neck a little fainter.
Just now another ounce of starlight streaks
into the atmosphere, ten million years
just to get here, & why we don't call that a miracle
is beyond me, or the way neutrinos whistle right through
our bones without a sound. A storm moves on, its carotid
flare & flash above another town,
the town in which the hour we lost between Chicago & New York
is changing its outfit in the ruined theater,
putting on a new face at the mirror, a face
we'll never see, now trying out its lines for the last scene
of its audition for another day, as it watches ants
the size of eyelashes move across the floor, gathering
the sweetness of the ruin with tongues too small
to be seen, in a slow migration toward ecstasy—
we study them to gain insight into traffic jams,
which is like listening to Chet Baker play his trumpet
because it reminds you to practice more diligently,
& not because it conjures a night parked above
the Devil's Punchbowl where you ask a girl
what she's thinking, & she says, I'm thinking
I love you. Not because it teaches you to be lonely
a little better, to preserve as best you can the fine edges
of the solitary. From the leafless maples a host
of starlings sweeps out as one body, the history of flight
in each bird, each hollow bone. I don't know jazz
from God's ribs, but if the speck in my eye divides the world
in two, re-leaves the oak & makes of them each a dragonfly
against the sun, if it makes of the morning frost
a cathedral in which someone's trying to pray
but the carillonneur doesn't know it—hammering the bells
with his fists—the words *hallowed be thy name* shorting out

as he's kneeling, thinking if I were a priest I'd be home by now,
thinking as he looks up at the trillium-shaped cathedral Jesus
how the hell did they build this place, as if from the inside
out, but there has to be a better place to pray, a glacier
drifting like a ghost ship, traveling the length of its days
to some nameless ghost town, nothing
to do but witness the ruins of stars & what becomes
of all songs & starlight, thinking if I've forgotten,
if it's been that many years & a little more, forgive me.

Nocturne Past Dreaming

Birds are following their cries in long arcs
above the earth, trailing our names in their wakes,
until they're little more than white sparks
above the horizon. Zen says the way back

will be unknown to you, if you do not go.
That there's no end to a prayer that has yet
to begin, that they follow grief as birds follow
their cries. What you'll make of the moonlight—

a thousand origami moths, a hundred blind swans,
a geisha writing a letter—is nothing compared
to what you'll make of your grief, how a body's absence
deepens a shadow. Led out beneath the stars,

you can trace the old stories in the lights, & from birth
to death see your own in the few that fall back to earth.

A Splinter of the Buddha's Tooth

White tongues of snowdrops, moonknots
                              & greased shine,
daytime constellations of the field
of memory & devotion,
                         where we lose ourselves
for a while if we're careful
or lucky, a field lit by little more than a stray cardinal.

And the rain that spoils everyone's picnic
sounds like a standing ovation begun
                              by someone barefoot & hungry,
winnows itself in the smallest air,
the blind rain that disappears as it creates your face by touch . . .

Let's say you laid down your ambitions
along with your tongue, because it only spoke

of want, that because someone left,
                              your breath was no longer
your own, let's say you wrapped your hands

like bread to give away
(isn't it funny cerements have the same waxy texture
                              as a butcher's wrapping paper?),
your scapulae like soap angels in a gift basket
for the new neighbors,

even the lines on your torso, wrong-hand calligraphy,
ripples that exhaust themselves on a beach with lions . . .

Let's say you gave long after it stopped hurting,
all that is horse & not-horse dusted away,
                         wouldn't you resemble the needle's eye?

Wouldn't they call you a moon,
the sidereal tidelong pull of your gaze

                               carrying fishermen & loneliness

to a sea luminescent with yourself,
                        & wouldn't you be lovely always,

nearby & just out of reach?

Portraits of the Artist with Montale

He's rubbing out a charcoal sketch of me

                  from the dog-eared *Book of the Missing*

with a spit-salved thumb
until I'm little more than a smudged print,
until the pentimento

resembles my shade,
its halo of absence full enough
for another life—

E l'ombra che tu mandi sulla fragile palizzata s'arriccia,
the shadow that you send out on the fragile balustrade is curling—

                              two dollars

for a salsa dance at the fichera,
more than any other dancer.
One man only wanted me

to sit in the nude
             & eat rose petals.
On my knees the next morning
how sweet the host on my tongue. It kills me

that the word "fragile" survives untouched

                      through three languages,

not a crack or a nick or a vowel missing.

Black thumb.

Each page casts its own curling shadow on the next one,
like one a thrown body throws.

A Parade of Ghosts

In the late evening as the storm finally breaks
over the town, as each head turns up
to the sky & umbrellas suddenly bloom,
a man walks out of the red brick pharmacy,
between two parked cars & into the street,
forcing a brown Volvo & a blue Ford half ton
to screech to a halt as he moves out into the road
& begins to walk down the street,
past the florist who loves daisies best, past
the town bank the mayor runs, oblivious
to the people staring from the sidewalk,
the woman pointing from beneath
a translucent umbrella at the man in khakis
& a blue tie walking in the rain down the middle
of the street, oblivious to the cars warily pulling
around him as if avoiding a pothole, until
he's walking outside his old high school, four years
of loving a woman named Jenn without knowing
what it was to love a woman. He continues to move
without knowing why, or how or where he first
started, trailing a dolphin's wake of failed hopes
& desires. When he reaches his childhood home
he sees his mother frozen in the living room window,
his father's handprint red upon her cheek,
his father's shadow falling into all corners of the house,
but he doesn't pause in front, nor in front of the next house,
where his best friend, who drowned in the reservoir
outside of town when they were eleven, stands
looking out her bedroom window upstairs, looking through
the blue curtains that were the last thing she ever saw.
Perhaps because it's taken him forty years to walk
these last three miles, or because his lungs are straining
as if he's breathing for the last time, he doesn't notice
them as they fall in behind him, walking toward the middle
of the night, leading a parade of ghosts that is the history

of his life, past the church in which he rose reborn from the waters, past the house he would have died in if he hadn't started walking, & into the life he had always imagined.

The Other World

And the other world He spoke of.
The liminal hint of it, like fireflies, a wing
in this world & a wing in radiance. Stars glinting faintly
on the Kanawha, constellating the ghostly gridiron
of St. Lawrence. Purple dusklight loosestrifed
beyond, & beyond that, filling the black glassware
of the river birches' silhouettes. Each draught
from them is of both worlds, this one so near
& passing, tessellations of honeycomb & gilded tile,
your clover-bright loss measured to the last
meadow. He who calls us beloved casts His nets
there, & look, they're like sunlight on a vineyard.
Hauled in with the wind, I suddenly want to put my ear
to the smooth flank of the rain. To put my ear
to your mouth so I can listen to the willows tremble,
their silver catkins gauzed with rabbit-soft fuzz.
The sweet cicelies ruffle their white plumage
as they mouth the soil. You, too, will be laid down,
taken up as xylem, shaken out as feathers, as ash,
your name the hum of the blue arcs the deer
leave in the air as they leap. Of the solace
of thorns, what could I tell you? Will you take comfort
knowing you will gladly give your life for the sake
of your thirst? When the body is laid down
in its longing—the mosaic of veins at our wrists & feet
patterned after dogwood blossoms, the pulsatile sun
beneath our ribs, the three-day darkness
between them—it's wound with the same water that bears
the day's ashes to a vanishing point west of west.

Self-Portrait of the Artist as Io

As sirens bay traffic to a standstill
a butterfly flits across the road, the yellow shred
of a child's raincoat quickens
in a shop window's reflection, then swallowtails
into the next one then beyond, the shadows
of powerlines like marionette strings running
right through him. How quickly one can turn
from one's own life. The light in my hair
is the light in the three-story pines at the edge
of the parking lot. How many gadflies
in a memory? Once I measured the days
by the olives that fell, the unremembered
close by, wheeling like blind bats at the periphery.
I was alone. Then the cloud passed through
me. The bloodpenny taste in my mouth.
Then the Egyptian blue of clear sky, blue
of an aqueduct, a dark tunnel of water . . .
I passed through the mockingbird's song
to the other side, where I was still falling,
rain clinging to my skin, dusk, I'm silver grains
of dusk poured out from a palm of water.

Portrait of the Artist with Dante

Outside the window that only gives to the east wind,
                                   last sunfall splayed on the sill,
you're shaking out birdseed onto the new snow,
looking up at the sky above Florence,
                              rosettes & riblines pressed into the clouds,

wing- & thumbprints amidst the phosphorescent patches
of plane lights in the cloud cover,
                              as one by one they ascend
& coalesce into the radiance.
What space did your body leave behind that night
as you rose, what shade of blue
                              did you leave in the air?
Chagall, I think, the blue of Chagall,
                              blue of his dreamers flying
above the towns they were born in,
the blue in the lips of a drowned man

who looks like he's been hung on a line to dry,
waving for the rest of his death,
                              hair washed in a marlin's wake.

Here a salt lake would surround the island of reeds.
I've yet to see it, & still dream of a reed
that will grow back as soon as it's plucked,
                           là giù colà dove la batte l'onda,
where the water laps the shore.
Are you still waiting, as I am, for a word to be spoken
over your life, for the blessing
                          of a hand's windtouch on your head?
Do you linger, near to the dusk as you can get,
because you hope to rise again, to watch it disappear
                              beneath you,
to dissolve in the silver birchlight of a new moon so near
you can feel it pulse in your chest?

Here Aurelius has never spoken, & the salt lake at sunset

                                        begins to shine from within,
as if suffused by a pink bioluminescent sargasso weed . . .

We'll go on waiting, watching the sky for a sign

                              in the wakes of comets,
for bodies & lights disappearing suddenly,
waiting for a wing to touch us

                    before we join the brilliance at last.

Sun Goin' Down Bad Luck Blues

for Ron Wagenaar

Green lightning jagged
                    on black asphalt,
the old Ford pickup sweating its coolant
like a horse hitched to high noon . . .

late evening in August, I'm speaking out of a dry mouth
in the driest month—no rain in days,
                                no hope of rain—
an echo chamber for the cicadas
in their new bodies,
                    in their new lives,

the sound of the yet-to-be resurrected
somewhere behind their song—
nowhere to go,
                  no way to get there . . .
late hour, moon disappearing in the west,
                              old dog, old trick,
the feeling that nothing is left
except the light on its fur . . .

If I didn't have bad luck,
                I'd have no luck at all,
my uncle used to say—he of the creaky knees & the old guitar—
some tune he half-remembered hearing

in a garage, or beneath the static in between radio stations
while driving somewhere outside of town,

maybe wondering which bad sign led to the bad sign
                                he was born under,
cottonmouth or catamount—
wondering while lightning flashes

in the distance, as it is now, the sparks
of tooth on nail, O Lord,

                    tooth & nail . . .

& You, Old Ghost,
at times little more than a beaded bracelet,
little more than a carving in space . . .

no wonder he's been on his motorcycle for years now,

looking for an answer on all of the roads

                          he's never taken,

no wonder we turn to star charts & tea leaves
with our questions about the what's-to-come,

trusting to the charms we've carried
since who-knows-when—
black die, gold horseshoe, cicada wing . . .

Even the king of the ghosts
wears a rabbit's foot around his neck,

                        & it's his own.

Deer Hour Gospel

It's always our sight that blocks us
                        from moving forward through
the prayer labyrinth, always our own prints that keep us
from retreating. In this hour the blind & the near-blind appear—

bats wheeling through the sundown milklight,
                                 moths tracing the sidereal paths
invisible in the air—
& the apparitions reappear in the treeline,
their dusk-brindled deerskins almost invisible in the white that bleeds through,

the white that flames their tails when they flee.
There are still services that offer silent prayer,
                           their silent passing
& the wake they leave,
because there are cries that cannot be voiced,
                             needs we cannot name.
And so we close our eyes when we pray to seek the blindness
that offers a window into the world,
                          & the world within this one,
sudden rain so fine it could be just a trick of the wind & the light,
                                     there & gone,
as the deer move off, through the silky wilds
                         of Queen Anne's lace,
through clover scatter-brushed in the grasses,
the long grasses that hold the traces of their passing

for a moment only, & beneath the old pear trees
already heavy with their suns,
with the cities of clouds the caterpillars

have spun for their tombs

                            as they move from this life & into the next one.
And we, with our rain-limned bodies, listening
for the echoes of our prayers to return,
to the aethereal bodies drifting so close

                                   & out of sight,
listening hard for the sound of our own disappearance.

The Way of All Flesh

Charlottesville, VA

The girl at the copy shop—all of twelve
or fifteen years old—holds the fifty dollar bill up
to the fluorescent lights to check its authenticity,
an action that seems as natural now as shaking hands.
I remember watching *Invasion of the Body Snatchers*
& casting a hard eye on those around me, wishing
I could check their hipbones for the right hologram,
or hold them up to the sun to catch the watermark
beneath their throatline. Turns out dealing with
sci-fi clones is the wrong thing to worry about,
it's disappearing yourself, having people from town
in orange reflective vests with walking sticks
in groups of four or six search the rail line,
the creek that runs behind the soccer field,
as they were this morning for Morgan Harrington,
last seen at a Metallica concert at John Paul Jones Arena.
What consolation have we to offer? That she sleeps here
young in a poem, the way she wakes when we dream
this land alive? If our waking says anything—as the tern strikes
its own reflection, as the wisteria's milk breath escapes,
as birds dodge the aethereal fishnet of shadows the pines cast
daylong, the net they make of the sunlight all of ten seconds old—
it's that the world that's returned to us is not the one
that was taken, that some are no longer here. A planeload
of Uighurs deported to China from Cambodia—
it's as if they vanished into a black hole, one activist said,
no one's heard a thing from them. They went the way
of the fingerprints on the rockets used to seed the clouds
over Beijing, particles of silver & fingerprint oil mixing
with water & ice, binding together & falling,
until there's new snow on your dark hair, on your face.
If our scriptures say anything, it's that the God of this world
not only has us numbered, down to each whorl on each finger,

but has each forgiveness numbered as well, meaning seventy
times seven & more, meaning we'll be able to add up the darkness
between our bones before His mercy. Small wonder
the Hebrew scribes washed in a river after encountering the name
YHWH, out of reverence for what they had approached.
Or that the skin on the arm springs back after a thumb
presses on it, yet in the ridges of light from the print the body
tastes the plum notes of the Sangiovese grapes those hands
have crushed, remembers a vineyard, coccyx a dead man's anchor,
the spinning jenny of the skull paying out vertebrae,
the exquisite vines of the ribs, translucent leaves of skin.
I mean this as a comfort to you: they are numbered, the missing.
The body remembers them, scent of jasmine, body
of dandelion seeds, they are close by, body of grape leaves,
dew-rinsed, close by, rising. They sleep young in the earth,
arterial light through the trees, they rise, sunlight glinting
on the snow on your hair, a vein for every river on earth
& one for the one half in heaven, they found her,
sternum a cross of ash over our hearts, *they found her.*

Dusk Hour Gospel *(Each Poem Is a Poem of Exile)*

Lightning-sparked Willow Creek wildfire
to the south, coursing through pinyon juniper, cresting mahogany
& pinwheeling sagebrush & scrub pines,

200 acres from 20 in a matter of hours,
smoke-shadowed wind,
                              ash & shinglegrit,
blowing through the descending web-shot dusk.

The city buses light up, each inch of them, cathedrals
on wheels with no one in them,
the drivers presiding over empty seats
                                        & lonely miles,
while my finger keeps a place in the *Book of the Missing*,
the single line of the errata
                        which says only *for city read white heron dying*.
Though I've never said it,
I owe everything to each person who's touched my forehead,
all of them a long way from this city of silhouettes,

which is rising, roofline & lone fencetop rooster,
the almost-invisible EKG chart line of the Oquirrhs in the distance,
where trailside the angels rattle their tails
                                        when you draw too close.
Now everything that travels through the dark begins to hush past,
like the mourning cloaks, thousands of them,

the sound of their flight a singing too high for us to hear.
This is the way the world disappears—

each bearing a small piece away,
each an ounce of the 240 pounds of sunlight that struck the earth
every minute today, to the ounce my father's body.

O the body of radiance. And the taste of blackberries
& the look of the sun on them. And our thirsts, however brief,

each hand, each blessing, the press so near of those beyond us.
If there's nothing left, there's nothing left to ask for,
save starlight enough to steer by on that last voyage.

PART II

The Litter Bearers

Zen River Travel

So you set off on the path
that begins between two cut ends
of a silk scarf on the day

everyone in the country calls in sick.
The highway becomes
a deer run, the shoeshine guy

watches the otters on TV,
their shiny black coats
like nothing he's seen before,

the bear from the circus
the only one on the bike path,
making a break for it, pedaling

like crazy in its blue helmet.
What are you after, money
or a reality TV show, a dance

or denim shorts named for you?
When you think of laying down
all ambition, you notice the barbs

on the blackberry leaf's underside
(as if it, like the world, sets a price
on its beauty). Snow settling

on a horse's mane.
Migratory paths in the air
you're looking up at. Rain

that never reaches earth.
Let the swallows unzip you,
contrail where there was a rib.

Let the river carry you out,
your shiny wet feet,
there is no voice

that can call you back.

Tulip Mania *(The New Numerology)*

The number of Confederate dead in the overgrown
weed-shot Virginia cemetery is, to the mile, the distance
back home to Iowa, where once, in a dingy one-horse bar,
she took my palm, & asked if I'd been born
November 15th—off by one, or else I was a little late
to the party, though she only cleared her throat
when I asked about the next date. And so one
can count the coal cars to measure the winter cold,
each fallen cardinal that flew into the sun
of itself for each dead language.
The mourning dove shedding its feathers in Pompeii,
an abacus losing its beads, counting down until
there is no song, the sky falling a feather at a time.
The hairs on the newborn's head with the amount
of jade brought in from the hills next year, the knobs
on the old dowser's feet with the sudden appearances
of swans. Wooden horses. The meteors on one's birthday,
or the day before, each ridgeline & wrinkle in my palm
whispering of a day coming too soon. And the tulips,
the tulips in the field across the street, the ten years
it took the seeds to weave their silk into flowering bulbs,
ten skinny years, ten years of silence. Now walk back
from the light that stole in on the two of you this morning,
on your one body . . . wasn't there a number
you kept counting to as you awoke? The number of kisses
last night & tulips in the bouquet? Didn't you
have the feeling that this could only happen
in this place, at that time, that you'd never have another
moment like that in a hundred tulip lifetimes?

The History of Your Life in a Hair Strand

In the Cold War spies would smuggle microfilm
in their molars, in hollowed-out heels & coins,
statues of Buddha that conjure up a moon buried
in a river, & now that a lifetime of photos fits on a memory card
the size of a penny, a slideshow of your life can be hidden
in places only a cavity search would turn up.
Yet if there were only one photo of you surviving—
the black & white shot at Pompeii, holding your empty palms up
to the flakes floating around you—I wonder to whom
you would entrust it. Or the last hair on your head,
which holds each poison & chemical
& kiss, a history of your life in each hair, which middle
of which book you would choose for that strand. The Song
of Songs is too obvious, the Hardy Boys too easy a read,
Nancy Drew too hard. It would have to be an Austen novel,
for the simple pleasure of envisioning the strand drifting across
the grounds of Pemberley, getting lost in the wake
of swans descending. And someone picking it up
in their peripheral vision as the sunlight catches it
would think of you, & the evenings you spent
waiting on the bench at the zoo for a man to arrive,
who would carry a copy of the *Post* & a single tulip, as promised,
& see you smile for the first time, with your beautiful teeth
that have always ached a little with their share of secrets.

"Raindrop"

is the program that predicts the casualties
& damage of a given bomb in a given area,
a guess as to how many the shockwave will whistle
through, whether it will reach the wedding party,

the child selling whistles, the woman
kneeling on a rug. This nameless village is only
a spot of ink on a map, yet peering down
you see the beautiful tulipiere of the sky

turning above, hear the nearby creek's green
thrushsound, so like your mother's song,
how she would sing with clothespins
in her teeth, then return through the throng

of weightless wind-rippled bodies, still singing.
The most we could want is only the courage
to make it too costly to someone, & so you bring
not her song but her silence to this village,

the best you can do, an absence left in you
by her absence, which now hovers
above the footprints in the dirt, then cocoons
the woman & child, her silence like a prayer

shawl touched by everyone. Someday soon
we'll meet in the middle, & I'll guess
by the look on your face that you're the one
who brought the silence here, as around us

the world goes on as it always has, & we have nothing
to say but *hello, her name was Lilli, it's raining.*

Elegiac Stanzas

for George Garrett

You might have taught me to love crows,
to give you a new name upon rising—

dated star chart, wheatgrass poultice,
aster's memory of water . . .
                               dearest,
I've cut the bloodroot's fleshy underground stems,
I've tasted its red sap. I drowse on a bed of its white flowers,

beneath the Dog Star's heliacal setting,
                                   following your heels in my sleep.

Who will hold our umbrellas, who will we shiver against?

Make a wreath of your shoes. Linger near the tulips' cups.
Leave a bright coin on top of the hydrant.

Missing keystone, body on air, body of milkweed seeds,
                                  drifting gondola . . .

In my dream you return, carrying a branch of sunbright forsythia,
swinging it before you like a censer, transfixed by the ashes

the waters carry.
A finger on the seam between wind
                        & the rumor of wind,

between tendon lines
bread crumbs send
                rippling across the water—

they cannot bear me up any longer.
I do not know who will hold

the torches to light the new path. You can only
wait, in a light that will not remember your face,

in a rain you cannot touch.

Gacela of the Wounds

Only a half moon tonight
                    drifting in a starless southern sky,
only the half-truths it offers—

better than a sharp stick in the eye,
as my father says, better the desires
we struggle against

than the listlessness that attends their absence . . .
light at dusk, venous light, a dark red
                          blued as if by skin,

no stars but the white catalpas
heaping their incense onto the flames,
the scent of Paradise
                  from outside its high walls.

Better to marry than burn,
St. Paul said, he of the second sight
& the slaked thirst—

which seems only half right,
since so much around us burns instead,
                      even the waters
we lay down beside,
that hurry elsewhere,

better its dark music, like the sound
                      of tail feathers pulling free,
the sound of a hieroglyph I know I've seen written somewhere—

graffitied on a subway wall,

                    tattooed along a clavicle,
or maybe inside the Court of Nine Petals,

                          one for every heaven—
the sound of a thirst
for a kiss that tastes

                 of the copper coolness of blood,
for a body we will know by its wounds.

Consolations of the New Day

Early enough to still blame insomnia, to hear the owl calling into the distances
between your breaths, to witness the Rorschach sweat patches settle on joggers'
abdominals like translucent moths. The plumber's only here to offer you a glass of
water & your lost wedding ring, he's already pulled the translucent rose in the sink
out by its roots—orange seeds & coffee grounds, our own promises & hair enough
to cover each one of Qin's terra cotta soldiers. Your skin's as mysterious as the swan's
song, as aethereal as sunlight through silt clouds that salmon stir up on the riverbot-
tom—the labyrinth of pipes beneath the floors we walk on is nothing next to the
miles of arteries & veins that hurry our blood along. For our consolation, the sharp
distal end of a collarbone pitched against the skyline, a cairn of a single stone in the
country of sleep. Fingerprints pieced together from sugar grains for our consolation,
& an Isis temple-stone pulled from Cleopatra's underwater city. For our sorrow, she
& Antony together, their tomb forever lost in the benthic currents. For our com-
fort the history of our survival in the burning staircase double-helixed through our
bodies, each dusk & rain featherprinted on the edges, cures for snoring (a switch on
the ball of the foot) & obsessions with kites & new moons (a button on the spleen's
promontory) on their topographies. For our memories the hollow the moon's halo
left last night, for our memories each language, the vital & the beautiful the same
across three languages, *aorta, oboe, gondola*. For our love the failure of each to name
each pastel in the red-winged grey sealight of early dawn, each color on the ribcage,
in the waking, in the departure.

Since You Asked

for Lisa Russ Spaar

The fake British accent was both a conversation piece & an unlikely way to pay
homage to those who have awakened out of comas with strange dialects, speaking
languages they've never heard. I could never explain the obsession with the water
ceremony—maybe there's something about walking into a new day bearing the
stigmata of water, a reminder of a translucent body, a perfect love. Did you see the
full moon last week, orange-blooded & beautiful? Did you wonder which hour it
begins to lose slivers of itself to shadow? I never made it across the bridge to Marin,
never saw the clouds lose their way in the moody afternoons, though it's sometimes
Alcatraz I think of when the impossible is mentioned. Like Lake Delhi, nine miles of
lake vanishing in a single day, or the story of the only survivor of both nuclear blasts
in Japan, what terrible & perfect luck. They're still peering into the ruins of smashed
particles, though when I held the ruins of her heels in my hand I understood some-
thing of our history, her feet ruined by ballet, which is to say ruined by beauty. Thir-
ty years before I noticed the grace of our arches, of a naked collarbone, a proscenium
arch above a stage that pulses with the memory of dancers. I've never gotten it quite
right. Like Degas, going blind as he painted his bathers. Leaving his failures for us to
marvel at. Collarbones like two small oars, ribs the ripples they leave behind. How
you can take an arch, give it wings, & call it *swan*. How you can take a palace, reduce
it to embers, & call it *making love*. The terrible & perfect luck of loving someone,
& watching them leave. May their names never leave us. May the names of those
who died like swans in their music never leave us, Townes Van Zandt, Eddie Shaver,
heartsick & beautiful, their names a litany so like a prayer, *our Father, our Father.* We
pray so that God & people interrupt our lives, so we can lift them up. Because there's
no other way to say these things. Because there's no other place, & we'll lose pieces
of ourselves no matter how we try to stay whole. Remember John Yettaw in yours
tonight, the man who swam two miles into Myanmar to reach Aung San Suu Kyi, the
man who swam *into* a prison. Remember that five prisoners who escaped Alcatraz
are still missing, remember that there's a way through, that we all might make it back
some day, think of the distances we might reach by water or prayer.

A Blessing

for Paul Guest

Never apologize for love or accordions, how each can conjure Doisneau's Paris, musicians holding umbrellas for their instruments, children walking across the cobblestones on their hands. Here in the Midwest it's children vaulting the fence at the town pool at midnight, climbing the skinny ladders welded to grain silos, swanning off bridges & ancient planks above old water-filled quarries, all for a naked kiss, or one above the town. Once I thought of love like the lights of a far-off city somewhere across the water, someone who knew my name & the date of my birth before I met her, or off by one. Instead I found someone who knows when I'm thirsty by the look of my eyes. Nothing ever prepares you for that meeting, or to suddenly hear the seasons turning beneath the skin, leaves falling so regularly we mistake the sound for the quiet whistling of our hearts. Whoever named seasons & thirsts practiced first on plums & horses, the fine bones no one's discovered yet, & rose petals. When the sound of their falling keeps you awake, wait for a peace, one that is like the wake of the quick-winged blur flitting through the cedars after the rain, a peace that feels like a hand outlining itself along your ribs. Wait for the blind moths to unhinge themselves from the shadow-tracery on your skin. Wait for a weightlessness that is like being passed from a bier of hands to the water, a thousand prayer lanterns drifting around you, each inscribed with the same name.

Preparing the Table

The hill to the parking garage behind the new million-dollar turf field
runs behind the theater building, where a woman blackens a table,

with a small torch, for the set of Oklahoma—a theater major
who can't sing or dance, but this is how her love bears fruit.

As I open the car door, a player cracks a ball into the net
on the grass field in the amphitheater across the tracks from the garage,

as a keeper on the turf field saves a similar shot on the field below.
Something about two soccer games going on at the same time,

a stone's throw from each other, none of the players knowing about it.
Joga bonito, Pélé once called it, the beautiful game. A train pulls in.

It's about to stop in Charlottesville, though the haggard faces staring out
could just as well be stopping in the Hague, no idea they're about to fall

in love with Vermeer's Diana in the Mauritshuis, that they'll go home to wash
the feet of their beloved after they see the nymphs washing Diana's.

And when they watch my brother play in goal for Ado Den Haag
against the hated PSV Eindhoven, they'll sing his name aloud, they'll murmur

mooi wedstrijd, beautiful game, as they drunkenly stagger from the stadium,
their train tickets still in their pockets, each thinking of a girl they once knew

in the town they grew up in, a girl not pretty enough or too sad to play
Laurey Williams. The train ticket I found bookmarked at Neruda's tenth

love poem is in the name of Jazmin Baily, Cordoba to Retiro, a poem
that is like hearing your name called for the first time. Like finding an ivory key

in a pool of moonlight. She's crossed out one of Merwin's translated lines:
"No one saw us this evening hand in hand while the blue night dropped on the world."

"Descended upon the world," she's written in dark pencil. Now we know
what we lack, one critic wrote after witnessing Ulanova dance for the first time,

at forty-six, the part of Giselle, a role thought to be far too demanding
for her age. Between my first step off the train from Stirling & my first step

into the Theatre Royal, the rain turned to mist on the Glasgow streets.
Perhaps it took watching Giselle dying anew & dancing in the afterlife

to understand the pathos of a ballerina in the twilight of her career
in a role that should have been beyond her body. The western world's first look

at her, perhaps the first English words ever written about her. A glimpse
of grace, a human bridge between the two warring sides of the world.

This afternoon I watched a newlywed Korean couple descend from a chapel,
a step at a time, while three other couples scattered handfuls of pink & white blossoms.

Now I know what I've been missing, he might have said when he met her.
When I return I listen for a few minutes to a house I thought empty

until the girl in the upstairs apartment begins the first of the Bach suites
on her cello. Rostropovich played the same song beside the Berlin wall

as the people tore it down—shovels, pickaxes, even bare hands.
Smashing stone with stone. Graffiti in every color, in uncounted languages,

falling to the ground, crumbling into fragments & disappearing in the dust,
as a language leaves this world each day. Rushing out of his hotel as soon as he heard,

offering handfuls of francs to a line of drivers outside, to anyone
willing to make the six-hour cab ride from Paris with an old man & his cello.

I wonder who I lack. The notes are the feet of geese running along the water
as they take off—now they're above the house, above the town,

now they're circling another line of Neruda's that Jazmin crossed out, the edge
of one of many circles. The two books she lent me are inscribed by

two different men with the same name. "After these words, there is nothing
left to say," reads one. Yes. Something as small as that, the one right phrase

that sets the table with blossoms & the charcoal of a name. As in sleep
we return to find a table washed in starlight, everyone we know

who has passed on already seated, waiting for us to speak all the things
we meant to say in languages we couldn't save. She's crossed out

"recede through": "*Always, always, you vanish in the evening, towards
where twilight goes erasing statues,*" Neruda will say for the rest of his death.

Gacela of the Bright Omen

for Courtney Kampa

The deer lie down & leave the forms
of their breathing matted in the long grass,
>> Braille the wind brushes across—

sleep of many streams, lungs of camphor, nameless ache . . .

That language will outlive us, the signs last longer than the stones:

a river a wolf crosses will taste of ash,
I once heard. Carry a mockingbird feather
& forget the way home, sleep beneath a wolverine pelt
>> & suffer a seven-year hunger.

If you hadn't once turned from a road
because a line of crows flew beside your car,
we never would have met—
>> is it one of those that nests in your hair

while you sleep, that leaves its tracks near your eyes?
I'm losing my sight, you tell me—

how long will the books keep their letters,
before there are no faces
>> to go with the names?

I look to the flames
>> that open pinecones,
at the heron's silhouette
>> crossing the spring moon—

what moon draws the blood from your lip?

We can only pray, in a little prayer of one syllable
that runs the width of a breath & the length of a spirit . . .

we can only smear a cross of ash
on each eyelid, & listen for someone to repeat our namesakes—

blackbird on the cattail, ghost in the sycamore, green cinder—

& wait for the dew to wash our feet,
for the deer to rise up, & leave, in the long grass,
$$\text{an imprint of our bodies.}$$

A Life Buried in Water

Just after ten feet of shiraz-dark asphalt
we turn off a county highway,
where solitary hawks roosting on roadside fences
                                       keep the miles.
On the way to the river
bursts of wind westdraft through purple linen
                                 unwrinkling from the redbuds.
Instead of the old hymns, it's the chatter of the narrows
glittering with whitewashed foam

beyond the placid shallows,
as we gather to lay down a life in the water.

The season rises from the river
                        as if from a litter to ascend
through a hole in the roof of the house
into morning air thick with the lilac's oloroso-sweet perfume,

six different birdcalls in its wake,
all saying the same thing.
                     The preacher, in his pulpit
of water, staggers with my father's seventeen stone,
as he struggles to rise with the waterburied body.

All of its days the willow will reach with its hair
                               for the body he left in the river.

I think the resurrection will look like this,
tinfall light downdrifting
                   through the swaying greenbudded branches

of the liquidambar, as if through the translucent swirl
of river currents. The impossible body appearing as suddenly as snow,
the only sound
               the warm wash of the deer's breath,

as it edges forward to nose one of the lower branches.

Six Prayer Kites over Rock Island

Night retraces its steps
from the river, pacing
chert-slippered, touching
the girandole at its throat,
leaving only hand prints
frosted on windows . . .

South wind's afflux heavy
with mimosa, the blue moon
silvering the earth into pear leaves
& tree roots veined in the yard.
Emblems of an absence here,
a pair of shoes at the door
& an extra setting at the table.

Salt spilled on the table like fantails
of snow, the voiceprint
of the swan's first song.
Some bad luck, we tell ourselves,
an unexpected current—
that's life, we tell ourselves.

No one's ever prepared
for the river's greed—
not even the moon is enough
shimmering in its depths,
nor the half-rotten rowboat.
Not the gold earring, nor
one red boot—

Nor the color in lips.
It's true, a death
hides here, as it hides
behind all lives, between

two moons, one
hovering just above a dream

Above withered fields,
the second moon setting
deep in the river. The wind
picks up & there is nothing
in the river, no moon,
not even a wing tip, only
the wet prints on the bank.

The Butcher with Nothing But Bones

You've heard this before, middle school
science, wasn't it, *glass never becomes a solid,*
but the guy next to you is saying something
similar, as he points at the Virgin trembling
in the stained glass, the high winds
of March, probably, or else something
else again. You've heard of the few grains
of comet dust on our lettuce, the history
of the solar system as a garnish on our salad,
how the wake of fine hair & long lashes we leave
will outlast us. How the oil that anoints our
departures, on banisters & door knobs,
on saint's toes & steering wheels, wears at the edges
of what we touch, as if we steal away with
some small part of everything, even the distances
we can never approach. And yet we're surprised
when the marble toe evanesces, or by the poison
the spider's line of radioactive dye finds when
it's cast into our bodies, as if the stories
of the secret moons hidden between our ribs
had never reached us, as if platelets had never
been a complete mystery. In longing the body
becomes lighter than rain, becomes transfigured—
as Georges Méliès showed more than a hundred
years ago in one of the first films ever made,
a conjuror & his assistant disappear beneath
blankets, explode into confetti, leap into the air
to become each other, burst into smoke & float away.
Only stop-gap special effects, the kind a clever
child can accomplish, but in their alchemical bodies
you can almost see the wind between our cells,
picture the radiolucent bones like the believers
dressed as skeletons at a Day of the Dead parade,
prayers for their ancestors drifting up, the deep lines
on their faces once the wrinkles they loved

on their parents' faces. That there is no end
to our longing is only another way of saying
there was no beginning, the familiar lines we see
in the only two faces now in the butcher's window,
faces who couldn't be us, no, who could never be us.

Curio

for Keenan Marie Kampa

Still mid-pirouette
she awakens, moon-pulled
         like the sea, anchored
by a spring that runs down through the underground rivers
                to the pagoda of ashes,

sentry to the gate the dragonfly stitches
in the air, frozen at a moment of triumph

like Canova's Perseus—the Medusa-head held aloft
               like a lantern in his hand—

no different from the pickled kidney
           or pomegranate in a jar,
the pinned blowfly or the death's head moth
beneath the glass—

and as you gaze at her in the cabinet—
through dusty panes arabesqued
          with fingerprints,

her figure chained mid-motion like a constellation,
like the Hunter forever fleeing
          the Scorpion a horizon behind him—

there's a quality of emptiness in her delft blue eyes
you've not seen before, as if she's realized

she's only a faint approximation
of someone else's life, as if

there's no place that does not see you,
as if you, too, are only an echo
                    in porcelain, a shade of Ulanova, a ghost

of a nameless queen, the cardinal's reflection
                              that sets fire to the river.

—*after Rilke*

Revenant

From above the depths a loon calls into the distance,
one last note on the last string of the lyre,
the cry of someone who has only half-returned

from the shades of the underworld with no one
beside him, a foot in this life & a foot still in the water.
When a loon calls from above the depths into the distance,

the next world's soot-filled apples are shaken from the branch,
the pomegranates of ashes split apart, the salt pillars
tremble. Someone who has only half-returned

from that world would recognize it, someone burned
by the voices in the fires, a foot still in the cinders.
When you call from the depths into the distance

above, it's a lament for touch, your hand on her cheekbone,
on her thigh, for honeysuckle scent thick as silk on the air,
it's the cry of someone who remembers wheat holding up the sun,

the mouth-feel of cold cherries, the rain's unending mantras,
the moon's horses a white wildfire on the sea. You'll hear
the loon calling to you in the depths from the glassy heavens,
the cry of someone who will soon descend again.

Film 101: Final Exam

1. How would you film your beloved as a city? What's in her ten thousand windows? Would you include the forlorn chess sets in the park where you love to lose yourself? The canals that carry your translucent form?

2. Compose a sequence of your death.

3. Sketch a scene in which you show how the river takes on the shape of the bodies it holds (include a tracking shot of a cannonball soaring bank to bank).

4. How else would you show—besides falling catalpa blossoms, a cathedral in the sun, a prayer labyrinth, five radiant wounds, fourteen dark stations—the ruins of your life?

5. In the montage of your beloved—at the Laundromat, looking back from the middle of the street, smiling in sunshine as she kisses her beloved—how would you light the shots so that her cheekbones remind you of the fountains in the city of your youth?

6. How would you fit Sean Penn's ego into a single frame?

7. How would you shoot the smallness of Tuesday morning, its first inch (include a tracking shot of snow descending, & one of a mouse ascending to the next life through the owl's talons, its lungs the color of wind through snow)?

8. Would you prefer to have the film of your life—to be screened as one long flashback during your last moment—directed by Michael Bay or a drunken donkey with a camera in its teeth?

9. Explain how you would film each ghost Ulanova passes through each time she leaps as Giselle. What would you give to the ghost behind Orpheus to stay a moment longer, the one he doesn't know is there, as he ascends out of one hell & into another?

10. How would you film the Quechua word that means the touch in the night that tells you your beloved is there? Seven words for snow you've never heard, without showing snow? The honeyed taste the fungus called *noble rot* leaves in wine? The shadows the pear blossoms outside her window scatter across her empty bed?

11. My beloved is ten years younger than I—if the actuarial tables are right, I'll die long before her—how would you show her already carrying my death like a burned filament inside her?

Survival Plans

Even if all the lights in town go out at once
& we can't find the flashlight, or the matches
from the hotel in Nice, there's still the X-ray

of the X-ray of your torso on the dinner table,
the ghost of your ribcage
                              a moon-rinsed lattice

still faintly luminescent, or there's the lilies
in the watercut vase on the baby grand,
each a torch bright enough

to illuminate the rice grain slipped
                              in a keyhole,
the one with the map to the cache
                              of sheet music to Saint-Saëns's *Le Cygne*
(Pavlova's ghost on the water,
                    dying in the dance
each time it's played),
the entrance to the kingdom of heaven
                              notched on the other side,
though it might be the size of a pomegranate seed,
though it might look like a cherry blossom . . .

though we might never find it.
Let the others worry about generators, diesel fuel, canned beans, water,

we'll look for the key cut from a swan feather
buried in one of the pools

of shadows scattered around the yard, a key
to the Palazzo of Many Arches
                    our two bodies form together.

The Disciples Question Their Yogi

for Eric Pankey

Who was your master?
I was disciple to the burned bridge.
I learned generosity from a sitar string, poverty from a wick.

How will we know you?
For you I become the unhooded Cobra with its riddles.
The Crane. The Noose you look through.

How will we know you?
By my breathing, which sounds of the earth when the hammers cease.
I will be the one walking between you & the humming of the locusts.

What will you leave us?
All forms are only grape skins over the infinite.
I leave you the hours of the Half Moon.

What will you leave us?
I leave you the forms of your breathing. The Bridge. The Corpse.
I leave you the fields for your prints. I leave you the movements of the bo tree's
    shadows.

How will we know you are our master?
By the gifts I bring: a thorn's half arch. The scored rake.
A handful of salt. An empty hand.

How will we know you are our master?
You will find yourself apprenticed to hunger.
To stone. To the arc of air between the stone & the temple bell.

What if we forget your teachings?
You will covet the things of this world: carnelians, orioles, prayer flags at dusk.
The prayer labyrinth has no path, only the path you make by walking.

How will we remember you?
Not by my empty bowl, which you will leave outside for the rain.
Not by the cup we shared, not by anything that I leave you.

How will you leave?
As the cup spills its fullness into the empty mouth.
Look: the overturned cup, a tongueless temple bell.

Deep Image Hall of Fame

Dandelion seeds drift across ten acres of ploughed land,
a galaxy of seeds floating over the blasted moonscape—

the shreds of a prophet's cloak,
the shards of a sword shattered
                              on a goatherd's staff,
a thousand words for light from the *Book of Changes*
spoken in this world for the last time.

If they ever take nominations for the Deep Image Hall of Fame,
I think I'll slip that one in the ivory bowler hat
they pass around to the vintners & the troubadours . . .

That Hall's run by a one-armed goldbeater
who keeps his treasure in this world, where moths & thieves
                                        & poets play,
who applauds each time you turn back to its exhibits,
to the ordinary places they're housed in—

those roadside chapels, the makeshift cairns
beside the tracks, memorials to outlaws & saints
jury-rigged out of lilies & rusted six-shooters . . .

Then there's the way the morning glories open
their white-and-blue silk trumpets to the dawn's first light,
or the evening star, big-finned & smoldering,
or the new moon that's rising
                              deep in the Yellow River,
rippled by a wind
faint as the whistling of a one-lipped man
heart-heavy & a little drunk.

The Joke

for Stephen Dunn

A man is telling a story inside a typical office.
It is almost the same story each time he tells it—
it always involves football, money, women,
or some combination of the three. Today
it was supposed to end with the priest,
the rabbi, & the intern's mother, but the man
halted when he said "I am," because the rabbi
was supposed to say it. He realized there are two
questions in those two words he doesn't know
how to answer. Then he said, "When I came to,"
except the priest should have said something else,
& he heard three questions implicit in those four words.
It's been years since he was afraid of the dark,
& longer than that since he's lain awake listening
to the night, to the crickets—which sounded to him
like someone whispering while flipping through
the pages of a hymnal—& the bullfrogs, who creaked
like doors that were never meant to open.
He remembers hearing something deeper during
those long nights, a silence beneath it all
that was like the hush between dreams.
It was like listening to a wick burning after
the flame had been blown out, like seeing
a pair of sandals beside a well, or crushing
the belladonna's purple flowers in one's hand.
The man telling a story hears a similar silence
between these questions, the kind
you hear after someone leaves for the last time,
or after a bad joke or the final "Amen" in a church service.
Everyone at the office thought the punch line
was coming, that the long pause was for dramatic
effect, but he wasn't sure who was telling the joke
anymore. He felt the panic tighten in his chest.

Would he hear these questions behind every word
of every joke he'd ever tell? And that silence, why
were there no words for that silence? He looked
around at the expectant faces & heard the crickets.
Someone whispered something. Someone else
was thumbing through the book of his life,
he thought, he could feel it. The water machine burbled
& he remembered the bullfrogs. A door had opened
into the dark. The man telling a story ran out of the office
& crossed the road, as the intern, heaving a sigh, finally
told the bewildered crowd how the priest & the rabbi
ended up with his mother in a church bathroom.

Orpheus amongst the Fishbones

for Sammy

Only a taste for the neighbors'
leftovers & a persistent love
of back alleys keep you from hurling
silverware or a cat or old shoes

or the moon like a cracked dinner
plate at the yowling tom, only the strange
affinities between you & this *tenore
buffo* & his three octave range,

his missing ear & his ratty tail,
the way he noses amidst the trash cans,
aficionado of garbage, for a leftover morsel
& then continues to moan his lament,

the broken syllables of *Eurydice.*
He pauses again as he climbs over
the garbage can & sinuously stretches
to the fence top, first the forefoot

then the hind, rehearsing the same tune
that parted the shades for the living
for the first time, that took him down
the staircase of ashes, the city lights glinting

like the torches that light the gray corridors,
now tracing the steps that took him
up into a world he thought he could never
love again, the light breathing of someone,

he swears, behind him again, but as he turns
there's no one there, only his rapt
listeners, who learn from his song that to ascend
from hell without her is to never leave it.

Other Equations for Velocity

Distance over time, or beneath it,
the exact equation—strange that the bullet
exploding through the apple (a paradiso of one),
the handful of monkey shit flung through the bars
at the gawking visitor, the kingfisher that falls
through flame & snow at sunset,
are subject to the same ribbon of numbers—
beyond him, yet inadequate for the speed
at which one life turns from another.
For the world to turn from the sadness of Tuesday,
for the pace of the moth steering by starlight—
like her forgiveness, the means beyond him, the end
a distance he can only look to. The shrapnel that once
whistled at the speed of sound now traveling
a half inch a year through his abdomen, leaving
a score behind it, a symphony of sixteenth notes,
an inscription only the blood reads. Each time
the metal splinter sets off an alarm at an airport
he guesses at the distance it will travel
on the flight, the thousandth of an inch between
New York & Tokyo, the infinitesimal movement
in the time it takes to turn a glass doorknob
(like trying to feel the spin of the Earth),
in the time it takes for the thought—maybe
they melted down a slipper to make this—to swim
its way to his hand from a synapse near
where the night meets the sea, if cradling it
he cannot help but think of the ball
of her foot—a paradiso wherever we are,
she once said—& the surgeries, her ruined arches
like white gates that open into a courtyard
where a salt statue dreams of dancing.

Lines for a Thirtieth Birthday

for Jane

No one knew who had forgotten
the cake, but then someone said
something about the tiny cicadas
in the grasses after dark, the frail net

of sound wrapping round close,
insistent. It was because the band
never showed up, & the magician
was asking everyone about his lost

rabbit—one guest saw it as a metaphor
of some kind, but he didn't mention
it again. What's lost in the translation,
between voice & ear? You gather

only what the silence allows you to,
the poem a history of everything
you've been forbidden to think,
the names you promised never to

say. *Time & light are the same
thing somewhere behind our backs*,
said the unwanted guest, *the shtick
of creation*, but this caused confusion

among the rest of us, & it seemed
to have nothing to do with turning
thirty. Besides, the phone was ringing,
the veal smoking, the entire mise-

en-scène quite different from all our
expectations. Just imagine tuning
the first piano, you said, or begetting
the revolution with Fidel & Raul

& the rest—this is the difficulty
of a new decade, the re-reinvention
of the self, & if there's no candles
there's no wish—*je ne vais pas nulle*

part, you sighed. Well, the uninvited
might be slipping out with our best wine
& silverware, & the birthday song
they pounded out on the battered

keys sounded like half an accordion
strangling three cats, but before you
mention the student who thought
Alex's song in *Clockwork Orange*

was Beethoven's "Night Symphony,"
& before you tell me that at the end
of every revolution a bewildered
king stumbles to the gallows at dawn,

I want to say that your two *no*'s
pull out as one knotted scarf from
the magician's mouth, & become
the *yes* the world dissolves into,

& I want to tell you about the high
passes in the mountains, the orange
prayer flags flapping in the wind,
a flag for every year of your life.

The Other Side of the Curtain

Like Samuel, I want to answer the call
even I don't know the voice, even if it's for a morning
sacrament attended by shadows & bells,

by the last of last night's snow drifting
on the north wind then disappearing
on the ground into itself, by a moth frozen

in fire in the single candle's mason jar,
perfectly balanced astride the black wick,
its wings preserved in the blue wax. From a scattering

of snow & ash a voice calls: *Despertad*, awake,
time for echoes to end & voices to begin,
admonishes Machado, the dead man who talks

to me in my sleep, the dead man I've apprenticed
myself to, who calls from the cathedral
of ashes, who was himself *aprendiz*

de ruisenor, apprentice to a nightingale.
Soon enough dawn will relight that candle.

Ankle-deep in the year's first snow, twin filaments
above my shoes where the skin shows,
shackles woven from the Shirt of Agony,

sun a spinning Catherine wheel through
the clouds' last shreds, morning light lemon-rimmed
& red-rhymed, while the morning's silence goes

the way of the geese, a raggedy procession
pulling the winter in from the north—
not like the gold thread, stitched & strung

inside & out through the landscape, shorn of voice
& bird-call but still somehow hymn-haunted
& hum-hung, a dew-salved thumb that touches,

that now strokes along the cello's one remaining
string. There's a voice on the other
side of the temple curtain, there's a hand pulling

at the end of the rope, landscape not just a lever
of transcendence, but Spirit-tinctured, the end
of fear the beginning of another fear,

the end of the road the beginning of another one.
I speak to ask you to speak, that I may
speak: *Just because we don't know the voice doesn't mean*

we aren't hearing it. Beyond the next hill, the sky
gets a little emptier when two coyotes begin
to yip, as if they hollowed out the horizon's gray

heart, & we stop pushing & look into the distance,
waiting for the end of a song that has no end.

Walking beneath the vast arches of the blue cathedral,
cold white ribbons bright about my bones,
I trace new prints—between the snow-limned maples

& the ice-shagged cedars, the lilacs crowned
once more with white blossoms, a cardinal
jeweled in one of their whitest reaches—until I run

into my own prints on the other side of the rails,
getting lost a kind of grace, the snow a palimpsest,
a one-page history of the morning, unscrolled

by those willing to lose themselves . . . the shackles deliquesce
as soon as they form, then re-ring again.
Shama, the Hebrew word for "listen," carries

an implicit meaning to obey, & when
tangible absences call me beyond the familiar—
paw prints the size of a toddler's hands,

a car length of gravel, water in the rocks, water
in our skin—I'll lace up my boots & ghost
out the back door, ear to the rail, ear

to the sky—then a trembling or the last echo
of trembling, then a tremolo or a fading pulse
or the want of a pulse in the silence that follows.

A moth lifts off from the rail,
sound of the bell leaving the bell.

Elegy with Two Lemons

after Dalí, *Still Life with Two Lemons*

Neither the book of moonlight nor
Death for Dummies has yet been written,
so we must turn to Machado again—

to make sense of this sudden absence,
to suffer the innumerable ceremonies
of loss, the grief that courses like ichor

through our limbs—*Walker, there are
no paths, there is only the path you
make by walking.* There are no new

trails for us, though—we begin & end
in the kitchen, beside a table with two lemons
on it, that light the room ceiling to floor.

The lemons are two pieces of coral
plucked by a seagull from a nameless
sea. They are the fossils of butterflies

snagged by a collector who turned mute
when he pulled them from his ragged net.
Sliced up, they lie like the chariot wheels

of a defeated general, the wafers pellucid
as the stained glass windows
in St. Basil's Cathedral, that allow

the light to shine alike on penitents
& saints. On the table they are as silent
& eloquent as the bulbs of a rare tulip—buried

a hundred years & a day before they flower—
as the crumpled sketches of one who tried
every day to sketch loss as best he could.

Their bitterness is watertight, they hold it in
past the first cut—one extra moment—
until the blade presses a little deeper.

Poverty is the fear of loss—but neither
the lock of hair nor the blood on the lintel
will forever throw the dark angel

off our scent. I'd as soon consult the chicken
entrails in the garbage or beg the weathervane
for prophecies as the tea leaves scattered

across the stove, or the cards on the counter.
Why not scatter that deck—let the hanged man
stare. We've moved like strangers pushing

stones—each with our own sets of hours
& keys—for too long. Pick the picture
frames up off their faces. Our prayers

may return in bottles, the dice of drowned men's
bones remain a riddle, & hope may be faint
as the light of a bitter fruit, but tonight,

in this kitchen, on the far side of a table
set for three, it's enough to glimpse the pale
hair about your face, to find you with my hands.

The Litter Bearers

Glimpse of sun between purple storm clouds
like the flash of a heel through a palanquin's

                silk curtains—
when they postpone the Desire Roundtable
because our guest speaker's sleeping one off in a baggage cart
in New York or Denver or Albuquerque,

maybe I'll throw that one out to the tenterhooked crowd—

or the way your ankles cross
at the small of my back, or how the tiger lilies
tiger the ditches

          after a three-day rain—

& to bring down the house, I'll bring up our trips to the north,
when each night we huddle together

as we witness the litter bearers carrying

              the slain body of Draco
higher & higher into the dark sky, their scapulae
like angels of bone heaved up against an ark

                  built for one, just one.

The Litter Bearers (II)

the constellation Scutum, "The Shield"

The sun drifts west in its balsa raft,
its Heyerdahl voyage beyond
                    the last of the Blue Ridge,
the end of its journey as humble as the beginning.

All the new rhythms are like the old ones,
                            heart-hallowed, heel-kept,
a pattering of rain the wandering eighth notes
of the first of the Hammerklavier, descending

& descending, accompanied by jay-chatter, the hum the sparrow hawk's wings

leave in the air. We are too much with us, I'd finish
if I hadn't forgotten where to start, late & soon

in the morning I've gotten it half-right again, following
my tracks back home to find them inlaid

with a set of smaller prints, the erasures I've left behind deepened
by an animal that knows me by smell,

by fear, lightning now fibrillating the clouds to the east,
followed by the faint tremolo of thunder
                        or hoof beats at a distance.

We live with the white noise of lives that have left us, while we listen for a light

that reaches the mole's eyes, the light by which we read
the bones of the living & the dead,
by which we remember their yellow hair,
                        their ashen hair.

What can we hope for but to deepen the fossae,
darken the willow's shade with our shadows,

our lives the two notes missing from both the Sonata of Rain
                                           & the Drowning Fugue,
each beginning with a half-breath & a deep hush . . .

their cadence timed to the steps of the litter bearers
treading the night sky,
carrying the dead king into the darkness
                                     on his burning shield.

PART III

Aubades & Nocturnes

Bat Hour Gospel

Last sun on the skeleton
                    of the unfinished skyscraper,
one ruin shining on another,
the streetlights paler on the street beneath
                                    steel girders like tungsten filaments.
Some left their sculptures half in stone,
weeping Mary, Thomas reaching for the wounds,
                                    because nothing
could be held close without the non-finito,
the pathos of buried feet, the half-formed scapulae
                                    awaiting its polished wingmount.
And so the marble might come to resemble the unsaid
(the body of grace so like the rain's radiant limbs),

a language with as many words for nothing
as for snow.

A tongue for the city of embers where I find myself,
for the scarab's city of white sand
                    & bone, two syllables of the *Paradiso*
for the naked thief hanging
on the cross, who humbled himself in his last hour.

For what remains unfinished in us,
                    breath & rest of days,
fontanels, & the noctilucent ribs
                    we thumb like beads in our sleep.

Unknowable Aubade

Adrift in the half-sleep of the half-moon,
the blue umbels of the streetlight outside
sway in the night's benthic current,
medusae swept on toward blue
horizons, a blue already dissolving into starlings
& dew on the grass, already becoming tomorrow's
pomegranates & Queen Anne's lace.
The space between the lights begins
to widen, husked by a dawn light
that tins the asphalt, reshimmers the rainbow
luster to the oil spill on the driveway.
What does waking mean to you?
The first sound of the world must have been the moan
of the waters drawing back from rock & earth—
as they recede from our bodies as we wake—
a murmur like our first words out of sleep,
that sound like *thyme rags stone hush.*
How strange to rediscover
we do not know the world, to weigh again
all that is taken against what is given back—
morning rekindling the cardinal's wings as it unwicks
the streetlights. And though no one is going to appear
as if out of nowhere to stand in their fading
nimbuses, & descant on the absences
we dwell in, to wish us on toward another
consolation, the world is given back to us again
as irises & horses, as bamboo stands & tides of corn,
as the last hushed vowels of the sleeping.

Early Hymn from Humpback Rock

Early-morning sun a mandala above the valley, its light buckshot
through maple & elm leaves, already stirring
the chlorophyll in its green cups.
                          Humpback Rock corcovadoes
the landscape, unsigned & unworded,

striped by a stream of water re-chameleoned
out of a logjam of ice & stones
                          that fishhooks
around a bend & out of sight,
every field it passes a potter's field.

It would take nine vowels purled & whistled
                                    out of a hundred tongues
to transliterate the watersound,
surf-slap like palm against palm, the dripping
of the small rain gentle as the sough
                          of sweet basil leaves falling
on a window sill . . .
                there's a sound or two coming from Desire's empty seat,
the one next to me, rinkside at the big arena
                          of Ding an Sich, where the unmeasurable

speaks to what's missing in us,
the half-finished & nearly forgotten
                          a yoke with a tin bucket on each end,
one filled with rainwater, the other
with pear blossoms.

Between knowing & unknowing,
we're never sure what we're trying to draw close to,
what we edge toward in the pew
                          or dream or twilight.

We can only bring our absences to the landscape,
                                lay the leaves of the high hill
on our eyes, & let the river run,
small mercies, springsink, its totemic underpull & tow
                                        still carrying the small sailboats
we released when we were children.

Nail Bed Gospel

The doctor's report can say comminuted fractures
                                        of the distal metacarpals
when it means bone splinters,
long mornings re-learning to button a shirt,
re-imagining the swoops & arches of cursive,

when it means a half inch of gauze between my fingers
                                        & your cheekbone,
the radiolucent fragments as radiant on the X-ray
as the fireflies in each darkness between the constellations
                                        of magnolia blossoms—
the belltower whispers of their drift,
their inch of brilliance,
                        quill ends burning through
from the other side. Evening's deep hush,
                                its deepening wingbeat,
its last light dissolving beneath marble slabs,
inside cypress boxes, dissolving into saints' relics,

turning the reliquaries gold, the bones to ashes
                                & the ashes translucent.
If they return at all—omnipresent, charged with the safety
of pilgrims, plumbers, & thieves—

perhaps the saints return as we see them,
hauling our prayers with their remaining ounce of ash
                                        wrapped in a crystal shell,
descending against the wind.
Remember the one who doubted
was the only one to feel the wounds,
                                who felt the night end
inside His palm, though we'll never know
how many times he returned to them

(in its wounds the body is burnished, transfigured
like a moon glimpsed through a body—

in my shock I saw my hand on the hand in the wound,
the torn crescent lunulae on the nail beds of the first two fingers
of my right hand

white-winged moths with bodies of a single black stitch
returning from a three-day night).

We remember only those we've touched.

Bayadère Notturno

Always so late in the evening
out of nowhere voices begin to carry
without us, downdrafting
                          from rooftops,
beginning their recitation of the names
                                        no one will say again,
voices we mistake for leaves rustling in the street,
for the sound of a second rain
                              dripping from the limbs
of lilacs, from honeysuckle vines . . .

always so late the feeling it's so late
elsewhere, as *La Bayadère* lets out—
the spirits of Solor and Nikiya once more reunited
                                        in the Kingdom of the Shades—
& you & I find ourselves
with the audience outside in the new dark so near,
descending the stairs

to the street like the rest of the shades to the stage,

always so late those hailing distant taxis
                                        or a new day or better luck
around the corner, for whom the night
is never anything but a destination,

too late in remembering the riddles
of longing they loved in their youth,
why do the grey petals float,
                              why does the night flee
from its beloved,
riddles we still ask
by touching each other,

are there as many terraces in its darkness

                        as there are in our breathing . . .

always so late the return
to the white gate, to the garden burgeoning
in our absence,

so late the splendor
of an unnamed moon leaving its feathers

                        in the limbs of the pear trees,

the return to the lives
we've kept hidden,

                    the voices that crest
when the music begins

in another room—there, & there
again, beginning faintly—

always too late our surprise
as if this should have been another night
& we two other people

                        leaving before it ends

Carnival Nocturne

Peanut shells crackle beneath your pink slippers
as you pace. The players begin routines of a different sort
long after the show is over, long after the spectators
return home, their caricatures slipping from their grasp
as they unlock the front door. Teeny the strongman
is calling the torn names in the phone book
he ripped in half, as Vasserot listens outside, smoking
a cigarette with his left foot, his arms a phantom
presence he feels each time he reaches for another can
of peaches. Karlov the Great has gone to bed
regretting his dinner, three light bulbs & a seven foot
feathered boa, while in the next room Madame Sossman
is about to win a red nose & a pair of floppy shoes,
unless Noodles can beat three Hangmans.
Monsieur LeBeau stands in the big tent, still listening
to the cheers of the departed crowd. His daughter
won't return his phone calls, but tomorrow
will bring a new town, with a different name & story,
where anything is possible, & tonight the stars' white flames
burn on their blue wicks—she's out there, somewhere,
the one you left behind on the Serengeti, in the night
that paces in a circle with its one black shoe, beneath wires
no one will ever see, the sickle moon's ivory
as beautiful as your tusks once were.

Domestic Nocturne

after a line by Stevens

How tranquil the night when the wind
is gentle, when it doesn't even stir
the ginkgoes' elegant fans. The dog slumbers
without a whimper, the stables are quiet,
the parted curtains lean in their stillness
like exhausted ballerinas. It's when the wind keens
its way through the pines that the horses stamp
in their stalls, the thrush refuses to sing,
& the silhouettes forget their vowels,
as if someone switches a diamond stylus
for a rose thorn, or the incisor tooth of a saint.
Then the ginkgoes' roots cry out with mouthfuls
of loam, the potatoes moan, like monks
in their sackcloth, the spider plants nod
their medusa heads, sunless & prayerless.
Then the windows are lit, not the rooms.
You climb down from your vigil on the roof
because in that wind the viaduct's arches
remind you of the fine cheekbones of someone
who left today, because it disappears halfway across
the river, the same river she crossed today,
& as you descend the shaky ladder—like an inelegant angel
en route to tussle with Jacob—to find the windows lit,
not the empty rooms, you hear the cello groan,
you hear a stirring in the umbrae—the many lives
who have walked these dark rooms before you,
who have left footprints in the shadows—
& although you once wondered what kind of blessing
you could wrestle out of a spirit, you realize
that being haunted is a birthright for those
who will never leave, a meeting of hollow hearts
with its own beautiful music, its own particular waltzes.
This inheritance is yours to claim, this loveliness of ghosts.

Sixth Finger Gospel

Blue Ridge blued by a sundown dusk
                                  aethereal as mist,
as the bankbound pines let down their roots
into the creek. Duck's head a green fuse
in the water, each drop it shakes off
                                    a sunlit moon-shadowed city,
a city where I meet you for the first time
each morning, where the new cathedrals
                                    are built with the languages we lose
each day, even when we're sleeping.
I don't know how to explain the dream
we shared the same night
                                    an ocean apart,
why the moonlight, a fire kindled in salt,
leads to an altar
                                    ten thousand steps in any direction,
something we feel like a phantom limb,
                                    phantom days,
altardark at the edge of all things.
It may have gone its entire life
without being seen,
the owl horned in a nearby fir,
                                    such sidereal longing
in-between the pulse
of someone waiting to hear it,
because nothing returns from its cry,
                                    no one was there when Orpheus turned
the day he climbed out of one hell & into another.
No one knows how to measure an absence,
                                    drop-sized, city-sized, or a song
that reaches the underworld.
Here's the first of the ten thousand,
cicadas' high drone in the trees
                                    like old clocks winding down,
the sound of their new bodies, their impossible bodies,

the bodies they'll leave behind
> when their song stops
& they move like the rinsed rainlight
through the spiked branches
> toward the translucent chute,
the opening in the air only they can see,
soon, like us, & soon.

Filament

Early evening. The only time of day the seeds
from a tree you'll plant in ten years are visible,
floating on the wind. People rise from their dinners
to watch from their second-story windows,
telling their kid to quit it already with the Abbado,
this is the time to improvise if ever there were,
just let the keys take you where they will. Peering
through a buttery Sauvignon with a bread crumb
sieve bottomed in the glass, at contrails pinking
as they dissolve, at a string of geese unspooling
from the giant geeseball Dahl should have invented.
At the spider webs, spilled light & sand dollar scaffolding,
glistening on the grass, on the boxwoods, a host
of starry parachutes. Remember the American
caught crossing into North Korea in your prayers
tonight. Remember those who have yet to find
what they wish to die for, but spend their lives
looking, like Jonah. They're the ones who in days
long past would bring everything they could
to the temple to be burned, once a year, to thank God
for everything they had. I love them for their faith,
for handing down Isaiah to me after three thousand
years, for somehow, miraculously, keeping his words
unchanged. The sound of the wakes their lives leave
behind them are like leaves stirring in their sleep to let go,
like the murmur of some lost thrush, though
you've never seen one. The evening will drown itself
in itself, like yesterday, the questions you've asked returned
as questions. I'm waiting for you to take your first breath,
tonight, to awaken with a verse on your lips, a verse you read
as a child, to move so easily through the world outside
that everyone's clustered around their windows, gawking
at the translucent body tending to the last shoots of light.

Nocturne of a Thousand & One Notes

after Robert Doisneau, *Un musicien sous la pluie*, Paris, 1957

Behind the musician holding an umbrella
for a cello standing upright in its case

a staircase opens above a vista of fog, a painter
close by, stroking a canvas despite the rain,

or because of the rain. He's not going to play,
because the way he's peering down the street

he's waiting for a taxi, or for someone wearing
too much lipstick, but surely he's played for audiences

less distinguished than a painter & a crow on the fence—
for the adulation of alley cats, for the rain itself,

for the loneliness he still feels years after the war
took his mother. He begins to whistle a tuneless dirge,

a song for an unfinished painting, for the crow—
Caesar of carrion, king of the grackle-colored litter—

for the night, cut from the same shroud
as its black feathers, unsearchable & comfortless,

for the rain which reminds him of the sudden storms
blowing in over the chalk cliffs & shingle beaches

south of Cap Gris Nez, a dirge for the hands that taught him
to play. Not even this song, accompanied by the pissmoan

of gutterwater draining into the sewers, will stir her fingers,
like dahlia tubers, but still he whistles rainlong

as if it's once again the war, & he's playing his cello outside
beneath a plane-scattered sky, the roars & drones drowning out

his stately adagios, but above the buzzing constellation sits Venus,
an argentine glimmering bright enough to see even at sunset,

bright enough to attract anti-aircraft fire, & once more
in memory the orange & yellow tracers blossom & hang in the sky

like a balloon race in which everyone keeps disappearing.

Nocturne: Exit Music for a Film

Headlights strobe through the living room window
in three-second pulses, all the time in the world
I have to see your face before the dark rills from the hollows
at your temples, the pool beneath your lips—a pool
I sound with a fingertip—before you disappear,
as if stepping back into your shadow, into your own umbra,
a watermark of yourself. Cézanne once began a painting
with the shadows, I remember, as my hand blooms
between your collarbones, a white poppy that opens
onto a field of red poppies, your breath riffling their petals.

When you go, take the water drop inside our kiss, take the soft saetas
of the afterrain, the petals of water falling
from the branches of the apple trees. Leave me
the questions you have about the world—how the purple & yellow flames
of the crocuses respark, how the hinges sing in a higher key
when the door opens than when it closes. Tell me about a thirst
clover dew will not slake, the demands of the cutbanks,
repeat your febrile prayers of the daylong fast. Show me your wick-kissed
fingertips, the need to portage. The hour bones wax,
the hour before the web is finished, the hour before you leave.

If I tell you how your collarbones glint—even in the faint
tin-light of the stars, like sycamore-built coracles
on a dark river—if I tell you they're as finely formed
as deer prints, that I traced the seven fine bones
of your ankle the way I would cuneiform at a desert-bound altar,
if I tell you that my careful brushwork at your shoulder
moves in time to the sonata you played a week ago, a sonata at the piano
of moonlight—forgotten twice before it was written,
its first note the sudden intake of a breath
in which I remember nights I should have known.

Thinking of Thomas à Kempis on a Fall Evening

Maple leaves cinquefoil shadows
across the lawn, the thumb- and fingerwork
                                        of a hundred hands,
as headlights will-o'-the-wisp
from the road, then across a river
the color of a salmon's belly,
                            iridescent ash
& cloud & cinders.
                        Keep yourself as a stranger
on the earth, he said, half a millennium ago—

& it's as a stranger that I look out into an evening
that will forget me as soon as I leave it,

as the Rhine has forgotten his face—
or was it as a stranger to the earth?

Lines of geese unstitching the sky like the first day
I saw geese, the sunset falling
in feathers, one red maple leaf at a time,
                                    pine trees hooped
by their own brown needles, auraed
                            by their past lives.
Learn to die to the world, he said,
& what I know of longing seems knotted with the world—
the ten desires for every sense
                        we start out with,
evening dew in the lavender,
goldenrod silvered
                    by the moon they're holding up,
the scapula's silky wingmount, the look of icebergs
                                    from ten thousand feet,
the Bach Suites—is it all of this we must die to?
Someday the boat of his relics will wash ashore
unattended, inlaid with the fingerprints of the faithful.

Someday we'll know how to untie the knot,
                                      & we'll drift,
clutching the tidewashed shells that hold our holy words,
shadowed by the starlight that shines
                                    clear through us,
parting the wind & the waves without a sound.

Unknowable Nocturne

You return to find the front door
ajar, the aster's white moonbursts
the only light in the foyer.
                              The sound

of their petals falling
will keep you awake again tonight,
or else you will fall asleep

in the hallway, between the room
of longing, a peacock feather nailed
to the lintel above its oak door,

& the room of melancholy, a sheen
on the wreath of crow feathers
hanging from its knob.
                              A few words

by lampblack, half-lives of half-lives,
their spittle & smudges blood-swiped
on a single page ghost-chewed

down to a spare wick. On the other side
the page catches fire, a glow
you catch sight of through the frost

trilliumed on the glass,
the windowpane now the bridge
spanning the canyon you crossed

the day you left him—
a smooth stone in your palm—
or the day after,
                    you cannot remember.

Reliquaries

Hsia Kuei, *Twelve River Views*

March, winter's bag end, stung by a wind
like a rattlesnake in a mailbox,
                              haunted by a zodiac
of disappearing constellations,
as Pyxis fades, then Canis Minor, the little dog,
heads over the horizon with the frost in its teeth,

until the black roots of the frost hang over the evening sky
then fall as a bitter rain,
unforgiving, eave- & gutter-sluiced,
                              street salt & dog sweat
& the petals of too-early blooms.

What is this evening the dark sleeve of,
edging a little farther from us,
                              & now swinging back
from where it was, a moment ago,
out of bowshot, out of eyeshot, elegant
& restrained as the ink of Hsia Kuei—

in his *Twelve River Views* what isn't there
is as carefully attended as what is,

his ink's indigos a shade darker
                              than the emptiness they're brushed over.

The shade a ghost-life I once held as it slept,
as the winds in the black gums
carried the gray soughs of replies
                              from the next life,

as they do each night,
though I've yet to ask a question, yet to begin
beyond *what becomes of us*, trail off
when I think of that life in my arms,

surprised to hear my voice
                              as the wind is startled by cattails,
by a scrap of crow atop a fencepost.

Do you know why we call them veins,
the rivers that wheel beneath
                              the earth, returning—do they return,
people suddenly beyond arm's
or prayer's length, who leave
                              sidereal handprints in the tide's blind haul,
who leave their looks
of longing on our faces, their lives
                              like the white streaks of stars
on hour-long exposures.

The body of darkness begins its long walk
across the water, its palms held out,
as a snow owl disappears
                              into the full half of the moon.
How many wings between you & this moon,
                                   how many seas
between you & the other side of your life?
No answers, only moonlight
& the words for alchemy we know as *prism, daffodil bulb, longing,*

only a night like a lost scroll
                              spread across the dark water

& lit by a pale lantern,
a night where you're only the umbra of a letter

you've spent your life crossing out.

How often you've mistaken *want* for *need*.
Gone out with a cup of coffee

& returned with a quarter cup of rainwater.
Tasted the orange your beloved handed you before dawn
instead of her mouth,

rounded by longing,
a moment that weighs less than rain
or prayer, but the world falls away beside it.

There's a stillness inside us that the rain breaks,
a stillness broken not into noise,

but into thousands of stillnesses,
as taillights azalea the street outside in long streaks.

Though none of us deserve it,
grace says we'll each have our day,

finally redeemed when we give up
all that we have & a little more.
How else could St. Gaspare walk untouched

through the rain
(his body transfigured when it was laid down in its longing,
lighter than the catalpa blossoms)?

We lay down our prayers
as the dragonfly lays down the mile of sun

on its wings
when it alights on the water
& joins the rest of the radiance on earth—
our prayers for the missing,

who each speak the same tongue.
We lay them down as the rain passes through
their bodies & freezes, falling as the year's last snow.

Look: something from the sky
feathering down, in which to leave an earthly trace of us,
footprint, handprint, wingspan.

The world is one of three petals thrown from heaven—
we know the other two
                            by their brilliance,
sun & moon, by their role in each creation story.

Nowhere near what the Buddhists call Big Mind,
maybe, but a little mind of the last light:

look through the shoes hung by their laces on a telephone wire
& see a V of wild geese crossing a river
                                        on the other side of the world,
river birches silhouetted on its banks—
until the river's untied, like a translucent obi knot,
                                        & hung down the door of a dam.
Maybe it'll be like stepping through this cataract at the end,
when you walk away from your body,
                                when the wind empties your hands,
& you step through
                    to find a catalpa tree in bloom,
each a white knot of water tied by grace.

Moth Hour Gospel

for Charles Wright

You open the *History of Longing* as waiters shake open
white tablecloths in the restaurant across
the street, one blooming after another

like an out-of-sync choir line
of ghosts, each lamp through each sheet
                                        a moon glimpsed
through the body of your beloved.

Boarding passes & hotel keys fall from the pages
as you look for your name,
the letters that begin
                I think of us constantly,
the mistakes we thought we made . . .
The evening unfolds, half-rumor
                                        & half-unfinished promise—
late hour, the pilgrims' last prayers
tied to an orange prayer scarf
                                in sight of the altar . . .
moth hour, gates swinging shut
as the honeysuckle opens
                        to the Nessus Sphinx & Hummingbird Clearwing.

The flyleaf says our hands never forget the feel
                                        of the bearded arrow,
a thigh's smooth bow-curve,
that your beloved will never lie down
without you. That memory is knotting our hair,

the step above the last step & the season's first snow
will receive us, the heat will never stop

       leaving our farthest reaches.

That the inch of rain in our throats keeps us—
& keeps us from forgetting the names

      of the drowned.

As the evening disappears into itself
something unutterable wings by,
hushed by its shadow

    like a doge before a moon
in a canal's black waters.

     Let's hope morning's reachable
by boat. Let's hope the doge remembers our names

before we push off, that he won't stop singing them
until long after we lose sight of the shore.

Reunion • Fleda Brown
Linda Gregerson, Judge, 2007

The Royal Baker's Daughter • Barbara Goldberg
David St. John, Judge, 2008

Falling Brick Kills Local Man • Mark Kraushaar
Marilyn Nelson, Judge, 2009

The Lightning That Strikes the Neighbors' House • Nick Lantz
Robert Pinsky, Judge, 2010

Last Seen • Jacqueline Jones LaMon
Cornelius Eady, Judge, 2011

Voodoo Inverso • Mark Wagenaar
Jean Valentine, Judge, 2012